SOCIAL SECURITY GUIDE

Essentials And Maximizing Your Social Security

Elmer C. Garcia

Table of Contents

Introduction

The government's Social Security program is designed to assist handicapped employees, retirees, and their families. Workers 62 and older with at least 40 credits earned are eligible for Social Security retirement payments. Your regular benefit based on your AIME cannot be claimed until you reach full retirement age. If you start claiming Social Security at age 62, you will only get 75% of your normal benefit if you are 67 years old or 66 years old. As you postpone receiving benefits, your monthly checks will grow somewhat until you achieve the maximum payout at 70.

The government recalculates your benefit after you have passed your FRA to reflect the amount it withheld. The Social Security Administration will examine your case. If it finds in your favor, you will receive disability payments for the duration of your condition or the remainder of your life.

Surviving spouses of any age who are providing care for the dead worker's handicapped or underage kid may claim survivor benefits. The Social Security Act, which President Franklin D. Roosevelt signed into law in 1935, is what gave rise to the Social Security program.

The program won't end in the next decade or two, but it's feasible that its advantages won't be as extensive as they are now. The Social Security Board of Trustees 2022 report projects that the retirement fund's reserves will run out in 2034. Tax income will be sufficient to provide 77% of the payments that are now slated to be paid. The Hospital Insurance Trust Fund, which pays Medicare Part A, is expected to run out of reserves in 2028.

CHAPTER 1: Guide on Social Security

Most people's retirement plans include Social Security in some capacity, but the program does far more than that. In a word, Social Security is created to help handicapped and retired individuals and their families by giving people who satisfy specific requirements a guaranteed source of lifelong income.

Here's a deeper look at the program's operation, the many Social Security benefits that are offered, and what to anticipate when it's time to file for benefits.

Workings of Social Security

The government's Social Security program is designed to assist handicapped employees, retirees, and their families maintain their financial security by collecting taxes from working Americans and distributing the money to those who qualify.

Normally, a worker must accumulate 40 credits to be eligible for Social Security, but if they pass away or become incapacitated before that age, they may be able to do so with fewer credits. A credit in 2022 will be equal to $1,470 in earned income, and you are allowed to earn a maximum of four credits per year.

If you've accrued enough credits, you may be able to claim Social Security based on your work history, or if the amount is more than what you're qualified for on your own, you may be able to claim spousal benefits based on the work history of your present or former spouse. In certain cases, dependent children and other family members may also be eligible for family benefits.

When you're prepared, you must complete an application either online or in your neighborhood Social Security Administration office. You won't start getting checks every month until a government agent has verified the facts in your application and determined that you qualify.

Social Security Benefits Categories

The three primary categories of Social Security Benefits are:

- Retirement benefits
- Disability benefits
- Survivors' benefits

Retirement Benefits

Workers 62 and older with at least 40 credits earned are eligible for Social Security retirement payments. Your average indexed monthly earnings (AIME) throughout your 35 highest-earning years and the age at which you start receiving benefits determine the number of your benefit checks.

Your regular benefit based on your AIME cannot be claimed until you reach full retirement age (FRA). If you were born between 1943 and 1954, your FRA is 66; after that, it increases by two months each year until it reaches 67 for anyone born in 1960 or later.

If you start claiming at age 62, you will only get 75% of your normal benefit if you are 67 years old or 66 years old, respectively. As you postpone receiving benefits, your monthly checks will grow somewhat until you achieve the maximum payout at age 70. If your FRA is 67 or 66, this is equivalent to 124% or 132% of your normal benefit.

If your income is high enough, receiving Social Security payments under your FRA may result in you having to return part of that money to the government. If you will be under your FRA the whole year in 2022, the Social Security Earnings Test will deduct $1 from your checks for every $2 you make above $19,560. If you hit $51,960 before your FRA in 2022, it will cost you $1 for every $3 you make beyond that amount. The government recalculates your benefit after you have passed your FRA to reflect the amount it withheld.

If claiming benefits based on your work history will net a certain family member more money than they are qualified for based on their work history, they may do so.

The following relatives are eligible:

- Spouses
- Ex-spouses who have not remarried after a marriage of at least ten years
- Children younger than 18 or, if they're still in high school, less than 19
- Children of any age who were incapacitated before the age of 22,

which is defined as not earning more than $1,260 per month in 2020, having a medical condition that causes significant functional impairments and is anticipated to persist 12 months or more, or ultimately end in death

- To be eligible to receive benefits, spouses and ex-spouses must be at least 62 years old. Spouses and children must wait until the worker starts receiving benefits before they may claim family benefits on their behalf.

Disability Benefits

Adults 18 and older who are unable to work due to a physical or mental condition that is anticipated to last at least 12 months or result in death are eligible for Social Security disability payments. Depending on your age at the time of your condition, you can still be qualified even if you haven't accrued 40 credits. Because your benefit is based on your average lifetime income, those who made more money while they were employed would get higher disability payouts.

When you apply, you must tell the government about your employment history and medical history, along with any pertinent supporting documentation. To determine your eligibility, the Social Security Administration will examine your case. If it finds in your favor, you will receive disability payments for the duration of your condition or for the remainder of your life, whichever comes first. You may appeal to an administrative law judge or ask for a review if the decision is made against you.

Based on a handicapped worker's employment history, family members can be eligible for benefits if they are:

- A spouse 62 years of age or older, or any age if raising a handicapped worker's kid or a child under the age of 16

- Ex-spouses who met the same requirements as spouses and were wed to the handicapped worker for at least 10 years but have not remarried
- Unmarried minors up to the age of 18, or 19 if they are still in high school
- any youngster who was crippled before the age of 22

Survivors' Benefits

Benefits for the relatives of dead employees who were eligible for Social Security are known as survivor benefits.

In addition, surviving spouses of any age who are providing care for the dead worker's handicapped or underage kid may claim survivor benefits if they are 60 years of age or older (or 50 years of age if they are disabled). Ex-spouses are subject to the same restrictions as long as they were wed to the dead employee for at least ten years and did not remarry.

Children of the dead worker under the age of 18, or up to 19 if still enrolled in high school, as well as handicapped children of any age if they become disabled before the age of 22 are entitled to payments. If the dead worker was providing at least 50% of their financial support before they passed away, their parents can also be eligible for benefits.

In addition to these advantages, the surviving partner or kids can be qualified for a $255 one-time death compensation.

Key Lessons

In the United States, Social Security is a government program that provides retirement benefits and disability income to eligible individuals, as well as to their spouses, children, and survivors.

Workers must be at least 62 years old and have contributed to Social Security for at least ten years to be eligible for retirement payments. Up to age 70, workers who delay taking Social Security will get greater monthly payments.

The amount of those benefits vary from person to person and is dependent on your average indexed monthly earnings (AIME) over your 35 highest-earning years.

If they satisfy specific criteria, surviving spouses, children, and those who are unable to work due to a disability may also be eligible for payments.

Brief Social Security History

The Social Security Act, which President Franklin D. Roosevelt signed into law in 1935, is what gave rise to the Social Security program. In 1940, the first checks were issued. The government changed it in the 1970s to enable employees to apply for benefits as early as 62 when at first it only gave payments to those who were 65 and older. Additionally, cost-of-living adjustments (COLAs) were put in place annually to assist Social Security to keep up with inflation.

Although the program has so far operated mostly well, many people worry about the future when there won't be as many employees to support as many Social Security beneficiaries. According to the most recent Social Security Trustees Report, the program's trust assets would run out by 2034, at which point it would only be able to provide 76% of payments to retirees and 92% of benefits to disabled employees.

Although the government has put out several ideas to guarantee the program's long-term viability, no concrete measures have yet been made. The program won't end in the next decade or two, but it's feasible that its advantages won't be as extensive as they are now. To be able to pay for the majority of their costs on their own, today's employees need to prioritize their retirement savings.

The Social Security System's Future

Some analysts have expressed worries about the sustainability of a system where fewer active workers will be supporting more retirees due to the aging of the U.S. population.

According to the Social Security Board of Trustees 2022 report, the retirement fund's (OASI Trust Fund) reserves will run out in 2034, at which point tax income will be sufficient to provide 77% of the payments that are now slated to be paid. The Hospital Insurance (HI) Trust Fund, which pays Medicare Part A, is expected to run out of reserves in 2028, at which time program revenue will cover 90% of benefits, according to the trustees' projections.

If such forecasts come true, Congress will have to find a means to close the funding shortfall, which might include raising worker taxes, cutting benefits, raising the retirement age, or a combination of these things.

What Benefits Are Offered by Social Security?

Benefits from Social Security are available to eligible retirees, disabled individuals, and their spouses, children, and survivors. Your past earnings are one of the elements that go into determining the benefit amount.

What Sets Supplemental Security Income (SSI) Apart from Social Security?
Social Security has a different program called Supplemental Security Income (SSI). It gives elderly or handicapped persons with

little to no income monthly cash handouts to assist them with their basic requirements. You may be qualified for both SSI and Social Security payments.

How Old Must You Be to Retire?

You must attain full retirement age (FRA) to be eligible for Social Security's full retirement benefits. Depending on when you were born, your FRA changes. For those born in 1955, it is 66 years and 2 months, and it progressively rises to 67 years for those born in 1960 and beyond.

Bottom Line

One of President Franklin Delano Roosevelt's most notable accomplishments was the establishment of Social Security in 1935. With more than 65.6 million beneficiaries, the program continues to be a cornerstone of most Americans' retirement. Benefit amounts vary based on income and job history. Those who have retired may be entitled to receive benefits, as well as their surviving wives, children, and parents, as well as employees who are handicapped and their family members.

Given that the typical retired worker payout is just approximately $19,000 per year, you shouldn't rely on the program as your only source of retirement income. It's crucial to complement it with additional savings and investments, as well as alternative retirement choices like an IRA or an employer-sponsored plan like a 401(k) or 403(b).

CHAPTER 2: Social Security Numbers

What Is an SSN, or Social Security Number?

A numerical identification code known as a Social Security number (SSN) is given to residents and citizens of the United States to monitor income and calculate benefits.

As a component of The New Deal, the SSN was established in 1936 to provide benefits for retirement and disability. The SSN was first created to monitor wages and provide benefits. Today, it is also utilized for other things including monitoring credit reports and identifying people for tax reasons.

In the US, people are required to present their SSNs to create bank accounts, apply for government benefits, get credit, make large purchases, and more.

Key Lessons

- To monitor income and decide benefits, Social Security numbers are numerical identifiers given to residents and other U.S. citizens.
- In 1936, the SSN was established as a result of The New Deal.
- The Social Security Administration issuing SSNs.
- You must submit Form SS-5 to the Social Security Administration to get a Social Security number.
- SSNs are open to unauthorized use by persons engaged in fraud and identity theft.

Workings of Social Security Numbers

All Americans, including citizens, permanent residents, and temporary or working visitors, have a Social Security number, with very few exceptions. Due to the SSN's widespread usage by companies and governmental organizations, even non-working residents (citizens and non-citizens alike) may receive one.

Section 205(c)(2) of the Social Security Act establishes the legal foundation for issuing a Social Security number (42 U.S. Code, Chapter 7, Subsection 405).

The Social Security Administration is responsible for issuing social security numbers and cards (SSA).

Nowadays, Social Security numbers are just a series of random digits. Before 2011, the numerals had a function, nevertheless. The person's birthplace or place of residence was indicated by the first three numbers in those years. The year or month of birth was supposed to be represented by the following pair of integers.

The Social Security Administration decided to make it a group number instead out of worry that it may be faked.

Although there have been several instances when two persons received the same Social Security number, none have been utilized before.

Brief History of SSNs

As was already mentioned, President Franklin D. Roosevelt created the Social Security number as part of a plan to aid American residents in the years after the Great Depression.

To assist Americans, particularly those over 65, to achieve economic security, Roosevelt signed the Social Security Act in 1935. This included monetary incentives that would be determined by how much money they made before retiring.

The Social Security Board was created to uphold the Social Security Act and maintain record-keeping standards. This resulted in the development of a unique nine-digit number that was given to each person in 1936.

SSN Component Parts:

Area Number

The area number is the first set of three numbers. It symbolized the nation that issued it. Depending on how many individuals need SSNs, states can have more than one number. Area numbers for New Hampshire range from 001 to 003, whereas Hawaii's range is from 575 to 576.

People on the east coast often have the lowest SSNs. As assignments shifted westward, area numbers increased. As a result, those living on the west coast often have the highest SSNs.

The area number was delegated starting in 1972 based on the zip code connected to the postal address (which isn't often the applicant's actual location) on the application.

The first area number assigning procedure included certain exceptions:

- Up until 1963, the numbers 700–728 were given to railroad personnel.
- American Samoa, Guam, the Philippines, Americans working abroad for American businesses, and Indochinese refugees received 586 each (from 1975 to 1979).
- The Department of Homeland Security was given the numbers 729–733 for its Enumeration of Entry program for foreign nationals

admitted to the country to establish permanent residency.

- 666 won't ever be allocated.

Group Number

The group number is the next set of two numbers. The range of group numbers is 01 to 99. They weren't always given out in order. Originally, they stood in for the batches of 10,000 numbers that were sent to a state's post offices to assist in SSN assignment. They arrived on behalf of the issuing agency.

Serial Number

The real serial number is represented by the last four digits of the third group. Within each group, they went from 0001 to 9999. There is no usage of the serial number 0000. SSNs started being assigned at random in 2011.

Throughout its existence, SSN use has also varied. For instance, in 1943, they were mandated to be used to identify people by federal government entities. Other significant occasions in the SSNs history include:

- The Internal Revenue Service (IRS) began using SSNs for tax reporting in 1962

- As of 1970, banks were required to collect SSNs from every client.

- In 1983, you had to provide banking companies with your SSN to open an interest-bearing account.

- SSNs were first printed on driver's licenses, birth certificates, and death records in 1996; they were later deleted from these documents in 1999.

- In 2008, legislation mandating the use of SSNs to identify people was repealed.

CHAPTER 3: Need For Social Security Number

The Need for an SSN

A Social Security number is crucial to possess since it is directly related to any potential future benefits from the US government to which you may be eligible.

An individual's annual income and the number of years they have worked are tracked using their SSN. Whether they are related to retirement income, disability income, or health insurance, these numbers are necessary to calculate prospective financial advantages.

Employers ask for applicants' Social Security numbers as part of the application process when they begin their working lives. They include information on the salary payments connected to each SSN and the deductions made for workers' Social Security and Medicare contributions to the Internal Revenue Service (IRS). Additionally, employers disclose this data to all states with income taxes.

Additional justifications for requiring an SSN include:

- To create a bank account or other kind of account with money
- Requesting a government loan
- To apply for unemployment
- As a tax return identification
- To become a licensed driver
- How to get a passport
- When signing up for Medicare

Obtaining an SSN

Filling out Form SS-5: Application for a Social Security Card from the SSA will allow you to request a Social Security number and the card that goes with it. The form includes instructions on how to get a new card, replace an old one, and modify or update SSN information.

The form includes a comprehensive list of prerequisites, such as proof of age, identification, and citizenship or immigration status in the United States.

A number or card may be obtained for free. A person's Social Security number may change under certain conditions.

Theft of Identity and SSNs

People regularly use their social security numbers to identify themselves and to apply for credit. They lack biometrics and depend on supporting paperwork to demonstrate their legitimacy. They may be used for fraud and identity theft.

One noteworthy instance of this is when the CEO of the identity theft protection firm

LifeLock used his SSN in commercials to demonstrate the efficiency of his business. Later, his identity was taken many times.

Legislators have been attempting to distinguish some actions from SSN usage, such as leasing an apartment or acquiring a hunting or fishing license.

If Your SSN Is Stolen, What to Do

There are things you should think about doing right away if you learn that someone else is using your Social Security number or if you lose your card.

Have a security or fraud alert added to your credit report and get in touch with the credit reporting companies (Experian, TransUnion, and Equifax) to make sure they are aware of the problem.

To report any suspected or actual fraudulent use of your number, get in touch with the

Social Security Administration. Discuss the replacement procedure if your card is misplaced. If your card has been stolen or your number has been used, notify the authorities.

Keep an eye on your credit reports for any instances of unlawful usage of current credit accounts or unauthorized account opening.

How Can I Check to See If My Social Security Number Is Being Used?

It is difficult to determine whether your Social Security number has been hacked. Numerous folks are unaware till it is too late. There are a few methods to be informed about any unexpected activity that could be connected to someone else using it, however. You may keep an eye on your bank accounts and credit reports, confirm your income with the Social Security Administration, and ask the IRS for tax transcripts.

What Can Someone Do With Your Social Security Number?

One of the most crucial pieces of personal information you will ever own, if not the most crucial, is your SSN. You must maintain its confidentiality because of this. If someone obtains your SSN, they may use it to apply for employment, create bank accounts, gain credit, receive medical care, and steal government benefits while posing as you.

If your social security number is stolen, what should you do?

There are a lot of identity thieves. If you believe your Social Security number has been stolen, get in touch with the Social Security Administration. The organization may assist in resolving issues with revenue. You must get in touch with your banking institution and the credit reporting bureaus if you have credit issues (Equifax, Experian, and TransUnion). To report any questionable behavior, you may also register complaints with IdentityTheft.gov, the Internal Revenue Service, and the Internet Crime Center.

How Can a New Social Security Number Be Obtained?

Fill out Form SS-5 and submit it to the Social Security Administration together with two papers that attest to your age, identification, citizenship, or immigration status.

What Is the Wait Time for a Social Security Number?

As soon as it receives the required information and paperwork, the Social Security Administration delivers each person their social security card. This may need two to four weeks, particularly if the administration is experiencing problems.

Bottom Line

A social security number, sometimes known as an SSN, is a special identification number connected to residents of the United States, including citizens. About the same time the Social Security Administration was set up (1935) to provide us with retirement and disability payments, it has been around since 1936.

The requirement for an SSN today extends beyond determining the benefits to which we are entitled due to the payments we contributed to Social Security and Medicare during our working days. It is necessary to get a driver's license, create bank accounts, apply for loans, apply for unemployment benefits, and more.

Your social security number is the key to receiving significant future rewards. Therefore, it's essential to safeguard both it and the card it's on. Make careful to only use it as directed by authority (and not simply when someone asks you for it).

CHAPTER 4: Top Ten Facts About Social Security

Workers may use Social Security as a base of income to create their retirement plans. Additionally, it offers crucial social insurance protection to both families whose primary breadwinner passes away and employees who become handicapped.

The Social Security Act was enacted by President Franklin D. Roosevelt on August 14, 1935, and it has been one of the country's most well-known, successful, and well-liked programs for eighty-seven years.

Fact #1: Social Security isn't only for retirement. Additionally, it offers crucial protection from life insurance and disability insurance.

In January 2022, more than 65 million Americans, or more than 1 in every 6 citizens, received Social Security payments. About four out of five recipients are older persons, while another fifth either got Social Security Disability Insurance (SSDI) or were young survivors of employees who had died.

Employees who pay Social Security payroll taxes get life insurance and SSDI protection in addition to retirement benefits:

In 2020, almost 96 percent of adults between the ages of 20 and 49 who had Social Security-eligible occupations had obtained life insurance protection.
According to Social Security's actuaries, it amounts to a life insurance policy with a face value of close to $800,000 in 2020 for a young worker with average wages, a spouse, and two children.

In case of a serious disability, about 89 percent of those aged 21 to 64 who had covered employment in 2020 are covered by Social Security.

Many individuals don't know how much more likely it is to become disabled or die before their time. A little under 7% of those who have just entered the workforce will pass away before reaching full retirement age, and many more will become incapacitated.

Fact #2: Social Security offers a progressive payout that is guaranteed and maintains pace with cost-of-living increases.

The earnings on which persons pay Social Security payroll taxes serve as the basis for Social Security payments. The greater their benefit, the higher their earnings must be (up to a maximum taxable amount of $147,000 in 2022).

Social Security payments are progressive; for employees at lower income levels, they reflect a bigger percentage of prior earnings.

Social Security payments are progressive; for employees at lower income levels, they reflect a bigger percentage of prior earnings. For instance, benefits for a low worker retiring at age 65 in 2021 who earns 45 percent of the average income replace nearly half of their past earnings. However, although being higher in absolute terms than those for low-paid workers, benefits for high earners (with 160 percent of the average pay) only replace roughly 30 percent of former earnings.

Many firms now offer defined-contribution plans (like 401(k)s), which pay benefits depending on an employee's contributions and the rate of return they earn, rather than classic defined-benefit pension plans, which guarantee a particular benefit amount upon retirement. Therefore, Social Security will be the majority of employees' only source of guaranteed retirement income that is immune to investment risk and changes in the stock market.

Once someone begins receiving Social Security, their payments rise in line with inflation, assisting in preventing poverty as individuals age. Contrarily, the majority of private pensions and annuities do not (or do so only partially) account for inflation.

Fact #3: For almost everyone in the United States, Social Security serves as a basis for retirement safety. 97% of senior citizens either get or will receive Social Security.

By paying payroll taxes into Social Security, virtually all employees take part in the program, and almost all retirees get benefits. According to projections from the Social Security Administration, 97 percent of older persons (aged 60 to 89) already receive or will eventually receive Social Security.

Numerous significant benefits result from Social Security's almost universal availability. All income levels are covered as a basis for retirement safety. It doesn't diminish or deny payments to those whose income or assets reach a specified level, which supports private pensions and individual savings. Because Social Security's risk pool is not restricted to those who anticipate living a long time, no money is lost through lump sum payments or bequests, and its administrative costs are much lower than those of private retirement annuities, Social Security offers a higher annual payout per dollar invested.

The administration of Social Security is particularly effective due to universal participation and the lack of means testing. Only 0.6 percent of yearly payouts are used for administrative expenditures, which is a far lower proportion than what is used for private retirement annuities. Means-testing Social Security would undermine many of these benefits while producing no savings because it would place heavy reporting and processing requirements on both beneficiaries and administrators.

Finally, the fact that Social Security is universal assures that it will maintain public and political support. The vast majority of Americans claim they value Social Security for themselves, their families, and the millions of other people who depend on it, therefore they don't mind paying into it.

Fact #4: Social Security payouts are not substantial.

Many individuals are unaware of how little Social Security payments are; in January 2022, the average Social Security retirement payout was $1,614 per month or $19,370 per year. (On average, elderly widows and handicapped workers got significantly less.) When someone retires at age 65 in 2022 with typical earnings throughout their working career, social security payments will replace around 37% of their prior earnings. As the program's full retirement age steadily increased from 65 in 2000 to 67 in 2022, Social Security's "replacement rate" decreased.

In January 2022, the average Social Security retirement payout was $1,614 per month or around $19,370 annually.

The majority of seniors join Medicare's Supplemental Medical Insurance, generally known as Part B of Medicare, and have their Social Security benefits deducted from the Part B premiums. These premiums will deplete their paychecks more quickly as long as healthcare expenses continue to exceed general inflation.

Additionally small by worldwide standards are Social Security payouts. When it comes to industrialized nations, the United States is slightly outside the bottom third in terms of the share of typical worker wages that are replaced by the public pension system.

Fact #5: Social Security affects children significantly.

1.1 million children are raised above the poverty line by Social Security.
Both elderly persons and their families as well as youngsters and their families depend on Social Security. In 2019, there were more than 6.5 million children under the age of 18 living in households that received Social Security benefits. In addition to those who lived with parents or other family members who got Social Security benefits, this figure includes roughly 2.8 million children who received their benefits as dependents of retired, disabled, or dead employees.

According to the figure, Social Security brought 1.1 million kids out of poverty in 2020. (The data in the graphic illustrates the entire impact of non-cash subsidies using the thorough Supplemental Poverty Measure. These numbers are not adjusted for underreporting. Nearly 1 million children were pulled out of poverty in 2020 by Social Security, according to the more traditional, cash-only official poverty indicator.)

Fact #6: Social Security helps millions of elderly people escape poverty.

Official projections based on the 2021 Current Population Survey show that all other things being equal, roughly 4 in 10 persons aged 65 and older would have incomes below the poverty level. According to these figures, Social Security payments help more than 16 million older persons escape poverty.

The official estimates of how dependent older individuals are on Social Security may be overstated, according to significant research on retirement income from the

U.S. Census Bureau that compares Census figures to administrative data. According to the report, without Social Security, 3 out of 10 older persons would have been living in poverty in 2012, and the program helped more than 10 million older adults escape poverty.

Regardless of the metrics used, it is evident that Social Security raises millions of older persons out of poverty and significantly lowers their poverty rate.

Fact #7: The majority of senior pensioners get the bulk of their income from Social Security.

Most elderly persons get the bulk of their income from Social Security. According to many studies including the Census Bureau research, it provides at least 50% of the income for nearly half of this population and at least 90% of the income for around one in four older persons.

Except for a few at the top of the income scale, most retirees make small salaries. According to research by the U.S. Census Bureau, the majority of elderly low-income Americans get very little, if any, pension income. The majority of families with retirees in the lowest third of the income distribution had no pension income. According to Social Security Administration research that includes correlates survey and administrative data, one in four of these families had an annual income of less than $20,000, and roughly half had an annual income of less than $50,000.

Fact #8: People of color need Social Security more than anybody else.

For those with low incomes and fewer opportunities to save and accumulate pensions, such as Black and Latino employees and their families, who experience greater rates of poverty both throughout their working lifetimes and in old age, Social Security is a crucial source of income. About 2.5 times as many older Black and Latino people live in poverty than older White people do. Older individuals of color have more retirement insecurity than older adults of the white race due to the large racial wealth difference in retirement. Employees of color are less likely to get workplace retirement plans and are more likely to hold low-wage positions with small savings potential. Age-related economic differences between older white individuals and elderly people of color are lessened in part by social security.

Beyond retirement, Social Security is crucial to families of color. Because they have greater rates of disability and lower lifetime earnings than white employees, on average, and because Black workers have higher rates of early mortality, Black and Latino workers get significant Social Security benefits. Black employees are more likely to become handicapped or pass away before retirement due to persistent racial gaps in health care availability and quality, as well as in access to food, affordable housing, high-quality schools, and economic opportunity. Additionally, Latino employees have longer average life expectancies than White workers and are more likely to become incapacitated, giving them additional years to receive retirement benefits.

Fact #9: Women notably benefit from Social Security.

Women need Social Security more than males do because they often make less money, spend more time outside of the paid job, live longer, have fewer savings, and get smaller pensions. Moreover, half of Social Security recipients in their 60s and 7 out of 10 recipients in their 90s are women. In addition, 96% of Social Security survivors' recipients are women.

Because ladies often live longer than men do, benefiting from the program's inflation protection, progressive benefit formula, and benefits for spouses and survivors is disproportionately beneficial to women.

Fact #10: Only minor adjustments would put Social Security's finances in good shape.

Since the middle of the 1980s, Social Security has accrued total trust funds of roughly $2.9 trillion, with the surplus revenue being invested in interest-bearing Treasury securities. As a result, it has been able to collect more in taxes and other income each year than it pays out in benefits. However, when baby boomers retire in the next years, Social Security's expenditures will rise.

The combined trust funds for Social Security's Old-Age and Survivors Insurance (OASI) and Disability Insurance are predicted to run out in 2034 if lawmakers do nothing more. Even if policymakers took no more action once the trust fund reserves are exhausted, Social Security could still pay three-fourths of the scheduled payouts by depending on Social Security revenues as they are collected. Alarmists who assert that Social Security won't exist when today's youthful employees retire either don't grasp or are inaccurate in their representation of the estimates. Over the next 75 years, the difference between Social Security's predicted revenue and its promised payments is expected to amount to 1.2 percent of the country's gross domestic product.

Politicians should focus on raising Social Security's tax collections to mainly solve the program's long-term funding gap. As the population ages, Social Security will take a larger portion of our country's resources; surveys indicate that most people are ready to sustain it by raising their tax payments.

Recent developments also support increasing Social Security payroll tax receipts: Since lawmakers last discussed Social Security's sustainability in 1983, the tax base has decreased, partly as a result of growing inequality and the expense of non-taxable benefits like health insurance.

Conclusion

The Social Security Act was enacted by President Franklin D. Roosevelt on August 14, 1935. In January 2022, more than 65 million Americans received Social Security payments. Employees who pay Social Security payroll taxes get life insurance and disability protection in addition to retirement benefits. The greater their benefit, the higher their earnings must be (up to $147,000 in 2022). Social Security payments are progressive; for employees at lower income levels, they reflect a bigger percentage of prior earnings.

For almost everyone in the United States, Social Security serves as a basis for retirement safety. 97% of older persons (aged 60 to 89) already receive or will eventually receive Social Security. In January 2022, the average Social Security retirement payout was $1,614 per month or $19,370 per year. Means-testing Social

Security would undermine many of these benefits while producing no savings. The vast majority of Americans claim they value Social Security and don't mind paying into it.

In 2019, there were more than 6.5 million children under the age of 18 living in households that received Social Security benefits. According to official projections, Social Security helped 1.1 million kids out of poverty in 2020. Most elderly persons get the bulk of their income from Social Security. The majority of elderly low-income Americans get very little, if any, pension income. About 2.5 times as many older Black and Latino people live in poverty than older White people do.

Older individuals of color have more retirement insecurity than older adults of the white race. Women need Social Security more than men because they make less money and live longer. Half of Social

Security recipients in their 60s are women. Politicians should focus on raising Social Security's tax collections to mainly solve the program's long-term funding gap, authors say.

www.ingramcontent.com/pod-product-compliance
Lightning Source LLC
LaVergne TN
LVHW050346160826
845677LV00014B/3827

* 9 7 9 8 3 6 1 6 6 9 1 8 9 *